EGYPTIAN ART

EGYPTIAN ART

General Editor
Francesco Abbate

Translated by
H. A. Fields

PEERAGE BOOKS

English edition first published by Octopus Books
This edition published by Peerage Books
59 Grosvenor Street
London W1

Translation © 1972 Octopus Books

Originally published in Italian by
Gruppo Editoriale Fabbri S.p.A.

© 1966 Gruppo Editoriale Fabbri S.p.A., Milan

ISBN 0 907408 17 6

Printed in Italy by Gruppo Editoriale Fabbri S.p.A.

CONTENTS

INTRODUCTION TO EGYPTIAN ART

MAGIC, FUNERAL RITES, AND PICTORIAL CANON

Egyptian civilization, with its many singular and 'unique' features preserved practically intact with scarcely a variation for thousands of years, exerted greater fascination and interest among the peoples of the ancient world than any other contemporary civilization. Its very longevity and conservatism (and apparent timelessness) appeared to be convincing evidence to the Egyptians themselves, as well as to the other peoples of antiquity, of an Egyptian 'primacy' or priority in the discovery and adoption of certain aspects of civilization such as religion and art, the cult of the dead, and astronomy.

Herodotus, who visited Egypt in the fifth century BC, also shared this conviction. He sometimes uses the phrase 'it is said that the Egyptians', but elsewhere he is more committed and backs them openly. Thus he states confidently that the Egyptians 'were the first to consecrate altars, statues and temples . . . to carve figures in stone . . . to determine the inflexible course of human destiny . . . and to maintain that the human soul is immortal'. Herodotus remarks moreover that the Egyptians are the wisest and shrewdest of people.

In the Roman world on the other hand, this 'myth' was largely disparaged. Thus, Pliny the Elder had no compunction in describing as a 'vain pretension' the Egyptian claim to have invented painting six thousand years before it appeared in Greece.

There is full agreement, however, on another aspect, and this point has been stressed by all the writers who throughout the centuries have concerned themselves with Egyptian art in any way, from Herodotus and Plato to Winckelmann, Milizia and countless others – namely the uniformity of the Egyptian style which remained practically stationary on the same level throughout its evolution. This is so marked that according to Winckelmann the history of Egyptian art seems like 'a great desert plain which can be dominated from the tops of two or three high towers'.

Among the explanations for this phenomenon suggested by the famous German archaeologist, the one on which he spends the least time and amplifies least is the religious background. Present day writers, however, consider this to be the main inspiration of Egyptian art, though the term 'religious' should be replaced by the more accurate and comprehensive term 'magical-religious', since magic was truly the main 'social fact' of ancient Egypt. This is magical art, therefore, as in prehistoric times.

But although its principle may be similar (the creation and invigoration of a new reality through the magic power of images), the motives underlying Egyptian magic are very different and its practice is much more complex, because of altered historic and social conditions (with obvious repercussions on artistic form). Whereas Palaeolithic witch-doctors would create their reality as required, with their images being used once only for a particular day's hunting, the reality which Egyptian artists were called upon to bring back to life was meant to be eternal. Death was to be overcome, and the necessary conditions created, to allow the dead man to continue living his life (in all respects similar to his mortal one) in a new setting, the tomb. 'May I be able in the tomb to eat, drink, plough, reap, fight and love' states the *Book of the Dead* (a compilation of rules of guidance for the deceased in the difficult world of the dead).

The speaker is not the dead man's soul (called *ba* by the Egyptians) which, as soon as it is released from the body, assumes the shape of a bird and flies away through the air, but his *ka*, man's *alter ego* or spiritual 'double' present in the body since birth. It is the *ka* which ensures survival provided that all rules and magical rites (performed by priests and embalmers as well as artists) are perfectly obeyed and executed.

To enable the *ka* to live once again through images with which it would identify, the artist had therefore to comply with strict and rigorous rules. He had to ensure that his figures were reduced to bare essentials. To make his figures eternal, the dead man's most typical features had to be reproduced. All that was required to individualize this prototype was a certain facial resemblance, with the dead man's name inscribed on his image (the magic power of names was a widespread belief in the ancient world). Instant realism would be entirely inconceivable owing to the problems that had to be solved by Egyptian artists, not only on the magical-religious plane, but also on the practical level.

Increasing demand and the creation of proper schools

and specialized workshops led to a rationalization of artistic output, guaranteeing prompt satisfaction of orders received, and the maintenance of a high level of quality. Output in the long run became standardized into basic designs and patterns. This engendered that characteristic canon which has never ceased to astonish all critics, both ancient and modern.

In paintings and bas-reliefs, heads are shown in profile, the eyes, the shoulders and the body from the front, while legs and feet are once again in profile. This is not only because it is easier and more convenient to produce an image in this fashion, but also because these are a person's main and most easily remembered features.

In statues, the frontal principle is dominant, and whereas in nature faces are asymmetrical, in Egyptian art they are constructed on symmetrical principles, with a vertical dividing line making both sides the same.

Therefore, Francesco Milizia was not exaggerating very much when he wrote towards the end of the eighteenth century that 'the Egyptians by law and custom were forbidden to alter the style of their predecessors'. The term 'law' here refers to magical-religious requirements, while the term 'custom' refers to the simplified and standardized techniques which Egyptian artists had invented. This was an excessively drastic judgment which did not (and in any case could not) take into account normal evolution and changes from which Egyptian art was not immune, but which easily absorbed those immemorial traits which make an Egyptian figure instantly recognizable. Obviously, there could be no lack of painting manuals. An inscription in an Edfu temple informs us of the

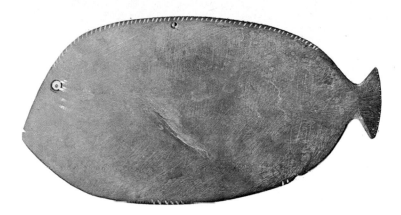

1 *Cosmetics trays. Predynastic. Louvre Museum, Paris and British Museum, London.*

1 *Cosmetics trays*. Predynastic. Louvre Museum, Paris and British Museum, London.
The slate trays on which the Egyptians prepared their cosmetics were initially fish- or moon-shaped. Later ones were adorned with designs of such complexity that they must have had ritual significance.

2 *Palette of the bulls*. Predynastic. Louvre Museum, Paris.
This palette celebrates the victory of an Egyptian king over some tribes in the eastern Delta. On either side, the king, in the guise of a bull, overcomes and tramples the body of an enemy.

3 *Cosmetics tray* known as the *Palette of the Dogs*. Thinite Kingdom. Louvre Museum, Paris.
The design is carved inside a frame of four mastiffs. On one side there are an ibis, a lion and a cheetah. The central cavity recalls the tray's original purpose. On the reverse side, two symmetrically placed giraffes stretch their necks to reach some palm-leaves.

4 *King Narmer's tray*. Thinite Kingdom. Egyptian Museum, Cairo.
Two heads of the goddess Hathor, adviser and protectress of the Pharaohs, watch benevolently over the triumph of Narmer who is about to slay a prostrate enemy. The god Horus hands over a captive Lower Egypt – the land of papyrus.

5 *Sepulchral stele of the 'Serpent' king*. Thinite Kingdom. Louvre Museum, Paris.
One of the finest and best-known stelae is that of King Wadji-Djet, a First Dynasty sovereign. The word *djet* means 'serpent' in Egyptian, and the King's name is exemplified by the serpent in the centre of the stele. The panel around it represents the royal palace enclosure, over which watch is kept by a hawk, sacred to the god Horus.

2 *Palette of the bulls. Predynastic. Louvre Museum, Paris.*

3   *Cosmetics tray known as the Palette of the Dogs. Thinite Kingdom. Louvre Museum, Paris.*

4 *King Narmer's tray. Thinite Kingdom. Egyptian Museum, Cairo.*

5   *Sepulchral stele of the 'Serpent' king. Thinite
Kingdom. Louvre Museum, Paris.*

existence of an instructions manual for mural painting, including the proportions which should be given to the figures.

The mummy and the statue guaranteed survival to the *ka*, allowing it to be reincarnated. The scenes painted or carved in the burial chamber recreated the actual conditions of the dead man's mortal span, and thus provided him with the possibility of continued life. Archaeologists refer to them as stylistically 'typical artefacts', indicating that a certain pattern and standardization can be noted in them, making it iconographically clear that these are not illustrations of actual events, but generalizations of common everyday events. The preservation of the social situation and privileges enjoyed by the *ka* in real life was absolute. Nothing changed after death in Egyptian society, and the artist's duty was to assure the *ka* that life in the tomb would be neither better nor worse than before.

Judges, for example, continue in office after death. Prince Masahti is guarded by a platoon of soldiers deployed in formation. The great men of the realm banquet, listen to music, enjoy pleasant conversations, and go hunting in a marsh specially recreated for them, while their servants play music, dance, serve at table, grind grain and knead dough.

In the most ancient times, to ensure that dead masters would continue to receive services, their servants were killed as well to follow him into the tomb. As this custom was obviously impractical and rather uneconomic, magic intervened to preserve the interests of the heirs and the lives of the servants.

By providing a wooden or clay model and pronouncing a spell over it, everyone was sure that the servant's image had been brought back to life in the tomb, to obey that master's commands.

Here, for example, is a dialogue between a master and his servant the *ushabti* (from the verb *ushab*, to answer), taken from Chapter VI of the *Book of the Dead*.

'O thou *ushabti*, should I be called upon or compelled to accomplish any sort of tasks which have to be accomplished in the hereafter, always make sure that the task falls to thee rather than to me, whether it be mowing fields, or filling canals with water, or shifting sand . . . I am here, Master, and I shall come whenever you command'.

Nourishment for the dead was assured by either depositing stocks of food, both real and in the form of images, or painting scenes showing the arrival of supplies. In any case, there was a simple formula which could be recited by charitable souls: 'one thousand loaves of bread, one thousand goblets of beer, one thousand oxen, one thousand geese, etc. . . for the soul of X'; stocks of victuals would thus be automatically refilled.

It may seem strange that in Egyptian society, which believed that artists possessed the power to perform such miracles, and in which art was not just a pleasant pastime but a primary and vital necessity, their actual social status was so low (as Winckelmann lamented, and as we know ourselves from ancient Egyptian sources), far below the status of prehistoric witch-doctors.

The fact was that craftsmen-artists were only material executants, bound by rules which they had to apply but which they had not drafted, as well as ritual formulas, the real significance of which they were

6   *Statue of King Zoser, originating from Saqqârah. Old
Kingdom. Egyptian Museum, Cairo.*

7–8   *Wooden*
panels from the
tomb of Hesyrê at
Saqqârah. Old
Kingdom.
Egyptian Museum,
Cairo.

6 *Statue of King Zoser,* originating from Saqqârah. Old
Kingdom. Egyptian Museum, Cairo.
The imperfect state of preservation of this statue does not
in the least detract from its regal power. On the contrary,
it curiously emphasizes the vigilant and imperious
presence of the King's glance.

7 *Wooden panels,* from the tomb of Hesyrê at Saqqârah.
Old Kingdom. Egyptian Museum, Cairo.
Eleven carved panels formerly lining the burial chamber
of the dead Hesyrê depict him in a variety of poses and
occupations.

8 *Hesyrê at table*, from the tomb of Hesyrê at Saqqârah.
Old Kingdom. Egyptian Museum, Cairo.
On a third panel from his burial chamber, Hesyrê is
depicted seated at table. Not even when dining does he
remove his insignia of rank. Various dishes are laid on the
table. According to Egyptian belief, so long as the dead
man's image was provided with food, his spirit could
continue to survive.

9 King Zoser's burial-place at Saqqârah : *Hall of Columns*
(top); *Enclosure walls* (bottom). Old Kingdom.
The great columns of this entrance hall are a reproduction
in stone of the clusters of papyrus which used to support
the ceilings of ancient Egypt. About 33 feet high, the
enclosure walls extend for nearly a mile, with salients and
recesses.

10 *Pyramid of Zoser* at Saqqârah. Old Kingdom.
King Zoser's tomb at Saqqârah began as a simple square
mastaba, only 26 feet high. The genial architect Imhotep
decided to overlay it with additional *mastabas*, achieving
a five times greater height with four gigantic steps. Still
not satisfied, he widened the base, increased the number
of steps, and the pyramid reached a height of 200 feet.

9   *King Zoser's burial-place at Saqqârah : Hall of Columns
(top); Enclosure walls (bottom). Old Kingdom.*

23

10 *Pyramid of Zoser at Saqqârah. Old Kingdom.*

unaware. The true creators were always the priests, or rather the magician-priests. Without their intervention, the images produced by craftsmen-artists, even though in accordance with the canons of art or magic, would have possessed no magic power at all. In fact, in contrast with artists, magician-priests were of crucial importance in ancient Egypt. This is proved by the tradition that records many magician-priests who were also princes of the blood.

One very tedious day, King Cheops assembled his sons, all of whom were experts in the field, and asked them to liven him up with a few tales of magic – this is the introduction of a tale dating back to at least the Eighteenth Dynasty.

The protagonists of one of the most pleasant of Egyptian tales (from the Ptolemaic era), which is outlined here because it illustrates certain aspects of Egyptian civilization, are two princes referred to as being among the greatest experts in magic of all Egypt.

Satin-Kharma, the son of Ramses II and an expert magician 'who had no equal throughout the entire land of Egypt', while strolling, as was his wont, through the necropolis of Memphis to examine its funerary inscriptions, is informed by a noble lord who suddenly appears in front of him that in the tomb of Nenoferkephtah, who was also the son of a king, is deposited a book written by the god Thoth (pre-eminently the god of magic, and greater than Isis, the 'great magician' herself) which contains two spells capable of conferring almost godlike powers on anyone fortunate enough to know them.

'If you recite the first spell, you will enchant the sky, the earth, the world of the night, the mountains and the waters. You will understand the language of all the birds in the sky and all the reptiles in the earth . . . If you read the second one, even though you may be dead in the tomb, you will regain the form you had on earth'.

Satin descends into Nenoferkephtah's tomb which is lit bright as day thanks to the illumination provided by Thoth's book, and asks for the book to be handed over to him. From Ahouri, the wife of the dead man, he hears the story of how the book was acquired, thanks to her husband's exceptional skills in magic, and the god's vengeance which caused the death of the entire family during their return voyage. Nenoferkephtah was buried in Memphis, while his wife and son were buried on the island of Copto.

But Satin insists on being given the book. The dead man then proposes a contest of magical skills with the book as the prize. Satin wins this contest handsomely, but primarily because Nenoferkephtah wishes to lose for selfish reasons. It was he who had appeared before Satin in the necropolis of Memphis and informed him of the existence of the book in his tomb (from which, thanks to Thoth's spells, he can emerge when he likes). By forcing Satin to take the book, he is able to punish him by sending him to Copto to collect the mummies of his wife and son and thus be finally reunited with them in his tomb.

Everything happens as planned. The dead prince's magical powers involve Satin in imaginary misadventures (which appear only too real to him). Feeling very sorry and frightened, Satin returns the book, and fulfils the wishes of Nenoferkephtah, who has also travelled to Copto to indicate the exact location of his wife's and son's tombs.

It was with the god Thoth that priests identified when performing the ceremony of opening the mouth (of mummies or statues) which was the culmination of all funerals, and was intended to make these effigies eternal. The very complex funeral ritual was modelled on the myth of Osiris, the god of the dead, and the circumstances of his death at the hands of his brother Set who desecrated his body and scattered the remnants. The god's resurrection followed when his wife Isis patiently gathered together his remains, as well as those of his son Horus, his sisters, and Thoth. In the god's resurrection, the dead man could see the certainty of his own, by means of the spells and enchantments pronounced by the celebrants reincarnating the protagonists of the Osiris myth.

Once the statue had been purified in various ways, and adored in expiation of the violence done to it by its sculptor ('O sculptors of the statue, stop doing disgraceful things to the father, do not strike the father, O sculptors do not transfix his body' – this was Horus speaking and these words clearly indicate that before the ritual started a statue was a purely material object), the opening of the mouth took place to enable the *ka* to enter and vitalize it: 'Horus opens the mouth and the eyes of the deceased as he opened the mouth of his father Osiris'. Finally 'he walks, he speaks', the dead man had become immortal.

At first, the privilege of 'Osirising oneself' was limited to the king ('as Osiris lives, the king lives; as he does not die, the king does not die; as he does not perish, this king does not perish' – from the Pyramid Texts). Subsequently, with the gradual democratization of funeral rites, every dead man became Osiris.

In ancient Egypt the power of magic was such that it

could succeed in deceiving even the divine tribunal which judged the moral conduct of the dead, and thus theoretically destroy the *ka* of the evil.

In the *Book of the Dead*, following a protestation of innocence and a pledge that no sins had been committed, it was magic that ensured the avoidance of all penalties: 'nothing evil will happen to me in this region, in the hall of truth, because I know the names of those inside it' and there were 421 of these. Knowing the name of something in ancient magic was equivalent to controlling it. And on the scarabs which symbolized the heart of the deceased, this spell was inscribed: 'Do not accuse me in front of the judges, do not contradict me in front of the one who holds the scales . . .' Thus, when the judges weigh you in the balance, in representation of my heart (an ostrich feather, symbol of Ma'at the goddess of truth, was placed as counterweight in the other scale), to check the truth of my claims, do not reveal my magical lies'.

Naturally, not all Egyptian art was funereal. There existed an art for the living of an official and narrative type (such as temple decorations, sometimes of enormous proportions, celebrating Pharaonic victories with a wealth of action and realistic detail). This ranged from a true decorative art in palaces to a minor form of art which was freer and less conventional. This included school drawings, sketches, notes, album pages or paintings now collectively known as *ostraka*. Many of these are animal figures ('artists were allowed greater freedom to express themselves when they were depicting animals' admits Winckelmann), statuettes of popular personalities, as well as figurines of servants to be placed in tombs (their somewhat courtly con-

11   *Pyramid of Sneferu at Meydûm (above) ; Pyramid of Cheops or Great Pyramid at Gizeh (below). Old Kingdom.*

11 *Pyramid of Sneferu* at Meydûm (above); *Pyramid of Cheops or Great Pyramid* at Gizeh (below). Old Kingdom.
The pyramid of Meydûm forms the link between the old step pyramids and the new pyramids. Sneferu's successors – Cheops, Chephren and Mycerinus – also built their own funerary monuments. These are the three pyramids of Gizeh. The biggest – that of Cheops – is 450 feet high.

12 *The Sphinx of Gizeh*. Old Kingdom.
The idol, with its incredible dimensions (242 feet in length and 65 feet high), was carved out of the living rock and only partly covered with carved stone facings.

13 *King Mycerinus between two goddesses*. Old Kingdom. Egyptian Museum, Cairo.
King Mycerinus, Chephren's successor, is holding hands with Hathor and Parva. This relief, carved in green basalt, comes from the temple built at Gizeh by the king.

14 *Small alabaster vases*. Old Kingdom. Egyptian Museum, Turin.
These elegant vases for perfumes and ointments were the pride of the potters and were produced for export to foreign courts.

15–16 *Prince Rahotep with his wife Nofret*. Old Kingdom. Egyptian Museum, Cairo.
The tomb of Rahotep, son of Sneferu, was located at Meydûm close to his father's pyramid. The prince's statue in painted limestone was placed inside it, alongside that of his wife Nofret, justly called 'the beautiful'.

17 *Statue of Chephren*. Old Kingdom. Egyptian Museum, Cairo.
Seated on a diorite throne, Chephren listens to the advice given to him by the hawk-god Horus, who is roosting behind his head. The interlaced insignia of the two parts of his kingdom are carved on the sides of this throne – the lotus flower, emblem of Upper Egypt, and the papyrus-reed, symbol of Lower Egypt.

12   *The Sphinx of Gizeh. Old Kingdom.*

13   *King Mycerinus between two goddesses. Old Kingdom. Egyptian Museum, Cairo.*

14   *Small alabaster vases. Old Kingdom. Egyptian Museum,*
Turin.

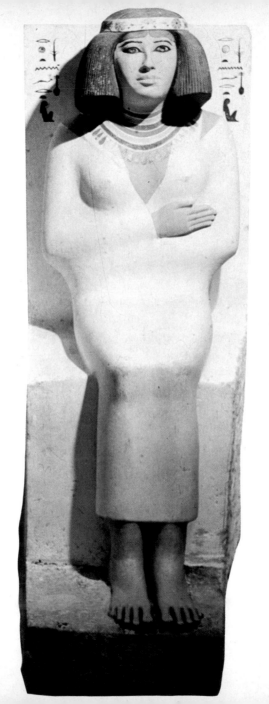

34

15–16 *Prince
Rahotep with his
wife Nofret. Old
Kingdom.
Egyptian Museum,
Cairo.*

17 Statue of Chephren. Old
Kingdom. Egyptian Museum, Cairo.

trolled style was dictated by the importance of the personality represented). It may perhaps cause surprise to discover that in this form of art unconnected with magical practices, we continue to find certain conventions and rules appertaining to funerary-magical art.

It often happens that the stylistic conventions, which, for objective reasons, govern the major part of artistic methods, are inevitably extended to completely different branches of art; unless of course there is specialization in the different branches of art – funerary art, secular art, etc. In ancient Egypt, the conditions required for specialization did not exist. What artist could be so irresponsible as to choose the most poorly paid kind of specialization (the secular form) and run the risk of dying of starvation?

Unlike literature, the figurative arts depend upon the existence of paying customers; and even though there may have been an occasional 'sceptic' – that is a painter who did not believe in magic or the hereafter – it is likely he would never have imagined it possible to paint otherwise than traditionally. The conception of 'art for art's sake' would have been unintelligible to him, and he could never have staged an artistic revolution. Painters could not aspire to the 'freedom' possible to poets:

'Therefore enjoy this beautiful day and do not weary of it' says the *Song of the Harpist at the Feast :*

'No one returns to tell how they dwell,
to say what things are needed,
to tranquillize our hearts until the time comes
for us to reach the place where they vanished . . .
See, not one has taken his things with him!
See, not one who has gone ever returns.'

18   *Memphis official with his wife. Old Kingdom. Louvre Museum, Paris.*

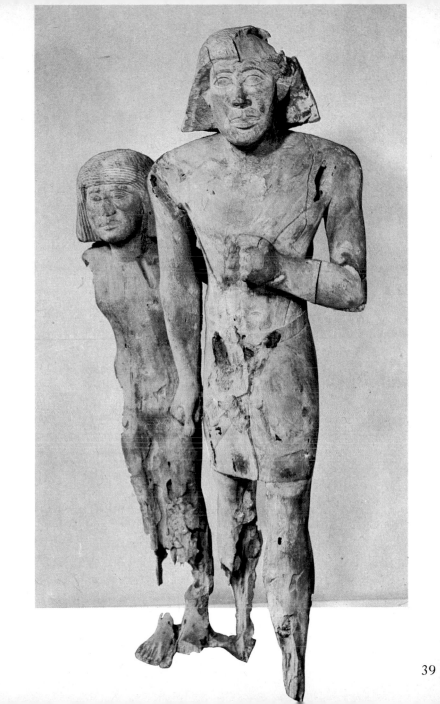

18 *Memphis official with his wife.* Old Kingdom. Louvre Museum, Paris.
Wood is a material very commonly used by Egyptian sculptors, especially for statues and likenesses of officials.

19 *The geese*, painted frieze from the tomb of Itet at Meydûm. Old Kingdom. Egyptian Museum, Cairo.
The Old Kingdom, which has such an abundance of spectacular architectural and sculptural monuments, is not so rich with paintings. This frieze, which is perhaps the most ancient wall painting we possess, was the lower part of a much larger painting depicting the netting of birds, the greater part of which is unfortunately lost.

20 *Scribe*, painted limestone statue from Saqqârah. Old Kingdom. Louvre Museum, Paris.
A massive figure, rigorously geometric in design and prodigiously animated with life. The scribe's attentive and concentrated expression seems to be designed to grasp his master's thought even before he starts dictating.

19   The geese, painted frieze from the tomb of Itet at Meydûm. Old Kingdom. Egyptian Museum, Cairo.

21　*Wooden statue of Ka-aper the 'village headman'.* Old Kingdom. Egyptian Museum, Cairo.
The Egyptian workmen who discovered near Saqqârah the wooden statue of Ka-aper, a Memphis official living around 2500 BC, spontaneously cried out: 'Look at him, he seems to be the village headman'. Since then, Ka-aper's image has borne this nickname.

22　*The dwarf Somb and his family,* painted limestone from Gizeh. Old Kingdom. Egyptian Museum, Cairo.
The realism of this painting of Somb and his wife, suitable for officials and common folk, is in complete contrast with the traditional style of portraying sovereigns and princes throughout the Old Kingdom period.

23　*Statue of Ti.* Old Kingdom. Egyptian Museum, Cairo.
From the tomb of Ti at Saqqârah. The statue shows Ti in the full flush of youth. The pure facial traits and the harmonious lines of the body produce an extraordinarily handsome figure.

20 *Scribe, painted limestone statue from Saqqârah. Old Kingdom. Louvre Museum, Paris.*

21　*Wooden statue of Ka-aper, the 'village headman'.
Old Kingdom. Egyptian Museum, Cairo.*

22 *The dwarf Somb and his family, painted limestone from Gizeh.*
Old Kingdom. Egyptian Museum, Cairo.

23 *Statue of Ti. Old Kingdom. Egyptian Museum, Cair*

THE OLD KINGDOM

The list of kings compiled by the Ptolemaic priest Manetho names King Menes as the reunifier of Egypt and founder of the First Dynasty, around 3200 BC. In all probability, Menes was the king who succeeded in establishing a stable and hereditary monarchy uniting the two lands – the Delta area (Lower Egypt) and the South of the country (Upper Egypt).

The struggles fought out among the various princelings prior to the final unification of Egypt, and even afterwards, are well recorded on early cosmetic trays. Beginning as common domestic articles for the preparation of eye make-up (which was ground and mixed in the tray's central cavity), these objects were gradually transformed into plaques intended to commemorate important political and military events. They depict lively and tumultuous battle scenes. The king, shown in the guise of a bull or lion, overthrows the walls of enemy cities, destroys, tramples and rends his enemies limb from limb. The animation of the narrative and the loose and relaxed postures of the figures shows us Egyptian art in an earlier phase than the more composed and 'rationalized' style of succeeding epochs.

In addition to these artefacts, descriptions of the struggles that were fought prior to the unification of the Two Lands are also found in religious myths – assuming these laws have been correctly interpreted. Horus, the god of the Delta and son of Osiris, takes vengeance against his father's murderer, his uncle Set, the lord of Upper Egypt, defeats him and deprives him of his kingdom.

The myth of Horus, the divine lord and first unifier of

the realm, who thus became the first national divinity for the whole of Egypt, gives us a glimpse of the unification of Egypt that took place in prehistoric times and was achieved by dynasties from Lower Egypt.

This first unification left such deep traces that when kings from the South recreated a single monarchy covering the whole of Egypt, they did so in the name of Horus; and the Pharaohs of the First Dynasty ruled the land on behalf of Horus, as his divine successors and reincarnation.

In King Narmer's tablet, one of the most famous, the king (identified as Menes by some critics) overthrows his enemy, while Horus symbolically presents to him a captive figure representing the land of the papyrus-reed, that is to say the Delta. King Narmer's tablet is also important from an artistic point of view. No trace is left of the narrative vivacity and dramatic animation depicted on early prehistoric tablets. The scene is simplified and reduced rather conventionally to a few ritual attitudes. This tablet gives an early indication of the distinctive traits that would remain the typical underlay of so much later Egyptian art.

Iconographically, Pharaoh is depicted as twice the size of other mortals, thus stressing his elevation above all other men and his divine descent. Even in the face of death, Pharaoh had to be distinct from his subjects. His tomb at Abydos, the necropolis for Thinis, capital of the two earliest dynasties, copied the construction and lay-out of the royal residence (known to us from the stele of King Djet, the 'Serpent' king, and impressive as a fortress) in accordance with the principle that Pharaoh's tomb was simply the king's residence in the world of the dead.

24   *Reliefs from the tomb of Akhtihetep, near Saqqârah. Old Kingdom. Louvre Museum, Paris.*

25 *Relief from the tomb of Ti, near Saqqârah. Old Kingdom.*

26   Relief, from the tomb of Mererukas near Saqqârah. Old
Kingdom.

27   *Relief from the tomb of Ti, near Saqqârah. Old Kingdom.*

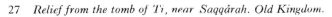

24 *Reliefs from the tomb of Akhtihetep*, near Saqqârah. Old Kingdom. Louvre Museum, Paris.

These reliefs from the tomb of Akhtihetep make us eyewitnesses to life in the household of a lord around 2500 BC. The scenes show preparations for a banquet.

25 *Relief from the tomb of Ti*, near Saqqârah. Old Kingdom.

Leaning on his staff of office, the official Ti watches the parade of offerings shown on the walls of his burial chamber. These scenes were made even more vivid with paint, of which only a few traces remain today.

26 *Reliefs from the tomb of Mereruka*, near Saqqârah. Old Kingdom.

The hunting and fishing scenes are particularly vivid and pleasing in the tomb of the *vizir* Mereruka (a *vizir* was one of the key-men of Pharaonic administration, being the head of the 'King's Household' or Chancellery, which coordinated bureaucratic activity). In these two scenes, a group of hippopotami are being attacked by hunters who are trying to harpoon them from their boat. In the second picture, Mereruka, standing upright in a boat grasps an animal by the tail, while nearby a herd of hippopotamus is immersed in the Nile.

27 *Relief from the tomb of Ti*, near Saqqârah. Old Kingdom.

Above, a herd of long-eared donkeys is trampling on grain which is to be threshed. Below, servants from Ti's household are building a papyrus boat.

28 *Entrance to the tomb of Ti*, near Saqqârah. Old Kingdom.

It was through this entrance, enclosed by two walls, that visitors passed bearing gifts to the tomb of the official Ti. Once they had crossed the enormous pillared entrance-hall, they would have laid their ritual gifts in the appropriate 'Hall of Offerings' decorated with extraordinarily rich reliefs.

28 *Entrance to the tomb of Ti, near Saqqârah. Old Kingdom.*

Court officials had to be content with less elaborate tombs, which externally take the characteristic shape of the *mastaba* (an Arabic word which means bench) with a rectangular ground-plan, upward-tapering walls and a flat roof.

The pyramid developed from the *mastaba*, passing through an intermediate stage represented by one of the most majestic and genial funerary monuments of the entire Old Kingdom. This was the Step Pyramid of Zoser, the Pharaoh who founded the Third Dynasty as well as the city of Memphis which from then on was to be the splendid capital of the Old Kingdom.

Described by Lauer as 'a gigantic sequence of steps rising into the sky to facilitate the dead Pharaoh's ascent to his father, the sun-god Râ', and by Woldering as 'the expression of the god-king's new will to power', the monumental complex of Saqqârah represents a fundamental turning-point in Egyptian architecture, as well as in Pharaoh's 'funeral policy'.

The enormous edifice was enclosed inside walls 33 feet high, surrounding courtyards, mortuary temples and halls of columns shaped like clusters of papyrus, this being the first recorded use of naturalistic columns in the shape of the stem and flower of a plant (the lotus, the papyrus, etc.).

For the first time, stone instead of mud-bricks was used to build an everlasting dwelling-place for a deified Pharaoh.

It was designed by the architect Imhotep, who was subsequently deified as a result (a really extraordinary honour for an Egyptian artist even though in ancient Egypt architecture was an 'honourable' profession and not a low-grade 'material' craft such as sculpting or painting).

The impression this complex gives is that of a composed and majestic calm and a perceptible feeling of timelessness, both pleasant and comfortable.

The life-size 'divine' statue of King Zoser (now in the Cairo Museum) with its tight cubical structure, is the prototype for Pharaonic statues with their motionless, hieratic, semi-abstracted pose. It implies not an absence of vitality, but rather a release from all irrelevancies, assuming an emblematic or symbolic quality which conveys the essence of the Pharaonic concept. To understand this point, the notion of *ka* is helpful.

It was only after Chephren (whose statue possesses the same abstract and imperturbable majesty as Zoser's) that greater attention began to be paid to the individuality of dead Pharaohs. This evolution towards true portraiture coincided with a gradual loss of faith in the notion of Pharaoh as god.

A further step forward towards the type of pyramid perfected by the great Pharaohs of the Fourth Dynasty is Sneferu's pyramid at Dahshûr, which has a square base, in contrast to the rectangular base of the Step Pyramid at Saqqârah. The original link with the *mastaba* is no longer clearly visible.

Cheops, Chephren and Mycerinus – the complex of their three pyramids at Gizeh eventually became the symbol of Pharaonic Egypt, its power and aspirations. The huge geometrical mass of the Great Pyramid succeeds, like no other man-made construction on earth, in conveying a sense of absolute timelessness, destined neither to decay nor to change, like the circumpolar stars to which it points so proudly, indicating that it is there that the dead Pharaoh has taken up residence, returning to the gods.

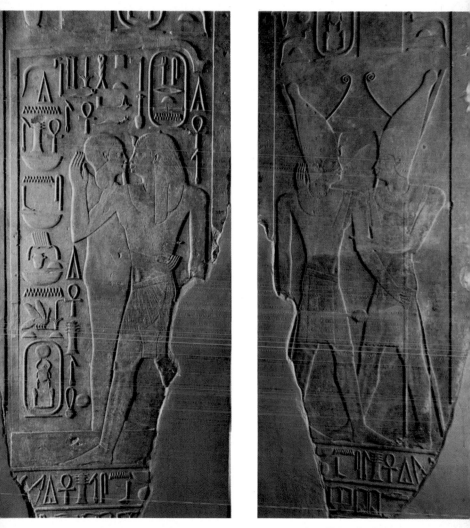

30   *Relief from a pillar in the temple of Sesostris I at Karnak. Middle Kingdom. Egyptian Museum, Cairo.*

29 *Sarcophagus of Rawer*. Old Kingdom. Egyptian Museum, Cairo.

The sarcophagus was the most important of all furnishings in Egyptian tombs. The dead body resided in it as in a house, protected from the sands of the desert, while his spirit could wander freely through the doors carved on its sides. Old Kingdom sarcophagi are shaped like palaces, complete with doors, windows, recesses and pillars.

30 *Relief from a pillar in the temple of Sesostris I* at Karnak. Middle Kingdom. Egyptian Museum, Cairo.

On the right, Sesostris I is conversing with the god Ammon. Neither his splendid appearance, nor his insignia, are in any way differentiated from those of the god, who is guiding him with benevolence and affection. On the left, Sesostris is breathing the air of life from the god Ptah, creator of the world.

31 *Wooden statue of chancellor Nakhti*. Middle Kingdom. Louvre Museum, Paris.

The wooden statue of chancellor Nakhti was discovered in an inviolate tomb near Asyût. During the Middle Kingdom too, the most commonly-used material for statues of officials was wood. The likeness is more realistic than in contemporary statues of rulers.

32 *Painted statue of King Mentuhotep*. Middle Kingdom. Egyptian Museum, Cairo.

The vivid contrasts of colour emphasize the vitality of the figure, which seems cramped in its ritual contemplative attitude.

31 *Wooden statue of chancellor Nakhti. Middle Kingdom.*
Louvre Museum, Paris.

32 *Painted statue of
King Mentuhotep.
Middle Kingdom.
Egyptian Museum, Cairo.*

The fascination aroused by the Great Pyramid must have been so considerable for the peoples of the ancient world that numerous legends arose attributing to Cheops great wickedness and cupidity. One of these legends, mentioned by Herodotus, alleges that Cheops compelled the entire people of Egypt to work as slaves in the construction of the pyramid, going so far as to prostitute his own daughter to obtain the money required to complete the undertaking.

The complex of tombs in the Gizeh pyramids, and subsequent ones as well, differs profoundly from the Saqqârah complex, both in spirit (a more liberal, varied and natural feeling permeates Saqqârah) and also in structure. The complex is centred around two mortuary temples, the smaller one being the 'down-hill' one which is connected to the true mortuary temple by a covered passage.

The Great Pyramid does not have any decoration. It was only later when unstable social conditions made it difficult to hold regular funeral ceremonies that it was covered with magical inscriptions (*Texts of the Pyramids*) in the name of the sun-god Râ to aid his son Pharaoh in his difficulties:

'I grant you the right to rise like the sun, grow younger like the moon and renew life like the Nile flood'.

Pure, carefully contrived mathematical-geometrical proportions are dominant in the Great Pyramid, because it also represented the Cosmos which was kept in perfect order and regular movement by Râ, the Heliopolis sun-god, who had superseded Horus as national god, in the same way that his son, Pharaoh, ruled his own terrestrial domain with eternal laws.

Around the tombs of Pharaohs at Saqqârah and Gizeh, stand those of their high officials who, even after death, would not abandon their Pharaoh.

So many were built at Gizeh that Cheops was compelled to issue decrees to regulate and standardize them. This cramped not only the style of their architects and the magnificence of the lords who commissioned them, but also limited space. Burial chambers no longer had room for statues, and these were replaced by surrogate heads, the so-called 'spare heads' which are sometimes real masterpieces of realistic likenesses enabling the *ka* immediately to recognize its material support without any need of inscriptions or designs.

However, once the restrictions imposed by Cheops were removed, along with the growing consolidation of the bureaucracy and the parallel weakening of Pharaonic power, during the Fifth Dynasty, the great men of the realm built magnificent and grandiose tombs for themselves at Gizeh and Saqqârah.

To these must be added the tombs built by governors of the districts, or nomes, into which Egypt was administratively divided; these became so powerful that their tombs come close to rivalling those of the Pharaohs.

With the gradual loss of their sense of the divine, Egyptians rediscovered life. The scenes of daily life lining the tomb of Ti (whose statue depicts him in the full vigour of eternal youth) are brimming with movement and action, conveying all the joy of living. Compare them with the conventional and restrained figures in the tomb of Hesyrê (Third Dynasty) or the arid lines of hieroglyphics decorating the table of Wep-em-nofret (Fourth Dynasty) in guise of offerings!

It was possibly the same reborn gusto for life that

dictated to a sculptor his extraordinary statue of the official Ka-aper (the 'village headman'), as stout and easy-going as a Tuscan farmer. Similarly, the geometric shapes making up the statue of the judge and nomarch Kai (the famed Scribe of the Louvre) are animated by an extraordinary tension, a controlled but vigilant and ready vitality, to the point that archaeologists have bestowed upon it the splendid title of 'living geometry'.

'Could I only make you love books more than your mother, could I only make you understand their beauty!' says old Duaf to his son while leading him to the Court school which will train him as a scribe. The scribe's is 'the greatest of professions . . . if one begins successfully, even though only a boy, one is honoured among men . . . There is no profession without a superior, except that of scribe. He himself is a superior . . . The scribe is protected by Ramenet, goddess of abundance'.

This is testimony which gives a clear picture of the scribe's social status, as well as the effective democracy governing enrolments into the Court schools which trained officials for the Old Kingdom, prior to the Fifth Dynasty when religious and civil posts gradually became hereditary. For instance, during the Sixth Dynasty, nomarchs assumed the title of Prince. Privilege became entrenched, imperilling the unity of the state and its traditional political-administrative structures.

During the minority of Pepi II, at the end of the Sixth Dynasty, Pharaonic authority disintegrated. Social conflicts became acute and the various nomarchs made themselves *de facto* independent. From the written evidence we possess, it would seem that a communistic

33 *Statue of King Sesostris III*. Middle Kingdom. Egyptian Museum, Cairo.
This is Sesostris III, the heroic Pharaoh hailed by Greek writers, and under whose leadership the Theban kingdom reached its zenith.

34 *Ploughman, in painted wood*. Middle Kingdom. British Museum, London.
Even in the tomb, the servant continues to plough his master's land. Magic spells were applied to these models, which were generally made of wood during the Middle Kingdom period, whereas terracotta was the material most commonly used under the Old Kingdom.

35 *The Gift-bearer*. Middle Kingdom, Louvre Museum, Paris.
The girl proffers her gifts to her dead master. This beautiful image provides a foretaste of the refined art of the New Kingdom.

36 *Head of Amenemhêt III*. Middle Kingdom. Egyptian Museum, Cairo.
Despite the mutilations it has suffered throughout the centuries, the head of Amenemhêt constit es a really outstanding piece of sculpture. The eyes, the traight-cut lips, and the huge and prominent ears, a cause the viewer's attention to concentrate on the ruler's enigmatic features. The oval fleshless face is topped by a very tall crown.

33 *Statue of King Sesostris III. Middle Kingdom. Egyptian Museum, Cairo.*

34 *Ploughman, in painted wood. Middle Kingdom. British Museum, London.*

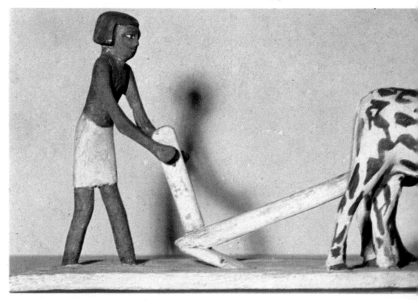

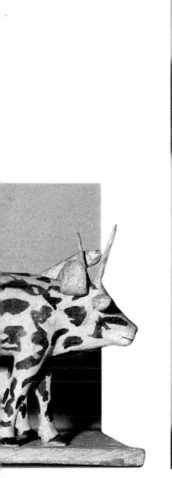

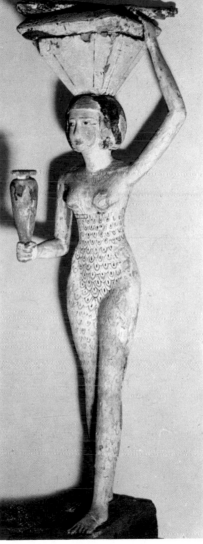

35   *The Gift-bearer. Middle Kingdom.*
Louvre Museum, Paris.

36   *Head of Amenemhêt III. Middle Kingdom. Egyptian Museum, Cairo.*

regime was established: 'The nobles are full of misery and the low classes are full of joy . . . gold, lapis-lazuli, silver and turquoises, hang on the necks of slave-women while ladies walk the streets wrapped in rags . . . He who once did not even possess sandals, today is the master of treasure'.

This 'lament' seems to be rather exaggerated and probably does not describe too accurately the disturbances with which the Old Kingdom ended. In any case, whatever actually happened, the feeling of insecurity caused by the upheavals of the period must have been so great that it caused an Egyptian poet (traditionally a lover of life and its joys) to sing a beautiful eulogy of death:

'Death presents itself to me like the aroma of myrrh, as when one is sailing on a windy day.

Death presents itself to me like the scent of lotus-flowers,

as when one is sitting on the edge of intoxication.

Death presents itself to me like a familiar road,

as when one returns from war to one's own home . . .'

THE MIDDLE KINGDOM

At the end of the Old Kingdom, the nomarchs, having become hereditary princes, exercised real authority over the provinces entrusted to them, and were virtually independent of centralized Pharaonic rule. From the struggles between various local potentates, there emerges the figure of the nomarch of These, Mentuhotep, the first effective reunifier of Egypt following the disturbances during which the Old Kingdom collapsed.

Even then Pharaoh's authority was no longer absolute.

There had to be a compromise with the remaining nomarchs, whose power was still great. Mentuhotep was no longer the god-king of the time of the pyramids, and he was not yet an absolute sovereign of the Twelfth Dynasty.

The mortuary temple erected by him at Deir el-Bahari – a blend of a traditional nomarch's tomb dug into the rock and the Pharaonic pyramid concept – also oddly confirms the nature of Mentuhotep's rule, half divine-Pharaoh and half-nomarch.

The singular temple of Mentuhotep, divided into courtyards and terraces, is one of the grandest and most graceful of Middle Kingdom constructions. It is certainly a unique work, but its 'human dimension' undoubtedly cannot compete with the superhuman majesty of the burial complexes in the age of the pyramids.

Throughout the entire Eleventh Dynasty period, the tombs of monarchs were not much more modest. Indeed, these local potentates seemed to have a mania for competing with their overlords, and it was only after the restoration of secure royal authority, during the Twelfth Dynasty, that the difference between the tombs of Pharaohs and those of their subjects once again becomes absolutely obvious. This was when Egypt's political activities extended for the first time beyond her borders. Sesostris I and Sesostris III began the subjugation of Nubia, an important gold-bearing region, extending the borders of Egypt to the second cataract of the Nile, just south of Abu-Simbel. Sesostris III also invaded Palestine and laid the foundations for a policy of penetration into the Middle East. Once again, their tombs are far more imposing than those built for their subjects.

37   *Mortuary temple of Queen Hatshepsut in the rock amphitheatre of Deir el-Bahari. New Empire.*

38 *Detail from Queen Hatshepsut's sarcophagus at Deir el-Bahari. New Empire. Egyptian Museum, Cairo.*

40 *Cosmetic spoon of the 'Swimming Girl' type. New Empire. Louvre Museum, Paris.*

39 *Relief taken from Queen Hatshepsut's temple
at Deir el-Bahari. New Empire. Egyptian
Museum, Cairo.*

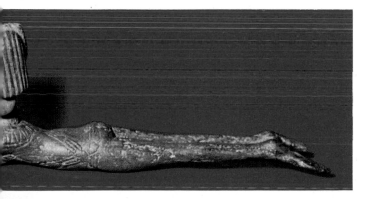

37   *Mortuary temple of Queen Hatshepsut* in the rock amphitheatre of Deir el-Bahari. New Empire.

For a while, Queen Hatshepsut's mortuary realm must have separated the world of the living from that of the dead. Not far away lay the thriving city of Thebes 'of the hundred gates', whereas behind it stood the Valley of the Kings, selected as their last resting-place by all the Pharaohs of the New Empire.

38–39   *Detail from Queen Hatshepsut's sarcophagus* (left-hand side); *Relief taken from Queen Hatshepsut's temple at Deir el-Bahari* (right). New Empire. Egyptian Museum, Cairo.

One of the most famous queens was Hatshepsut. She sponsored the construction of splendid buildings dedicated to the god Ammon.

40   *Cosmetic spoon of the 'Swimming Girl' type.* New Empire. Louvre Museum, Paris.

The figure of a girl, carved in wood, holds a duck in her outstretched arms. The duck's hollowed-out body contained cosmetic substances used by Egyptian ladies.

41   *Temple sacred to the triad of Ammon, Mut and Hons,* at Luxor. New Empire.

The temple of Luxor, consecrated to Ammon, his wife Mut, and his son Hons, was begun by Amenophis III, and completed by Ramses II. The various parts of the complex therefore reveal differing conceptions. The entrance-hall of Amenophis III (top) exudes elegance with its lotus-bud columns, The courtyard of Ramses II (bottom) gives an impression of power.

42   *Colossi of Memnon* at Thebes. New Empire.

The Colossi of Memnon are all that remain of Amenophis III's mortuary temple. Legend claimed that the Colossi represented Memnon, son of Aurora, who hailed his mother each morning at daybreak. Actually, these statues depict Amenophis III and the plaintive sound they produce is caused by the breeze rustling through them.

41   *Temple sacred to the triad of Ammon, Mut and Hons, at Luxor. New Empire.*

42   *Colossi of Memnon at Thebes. New Empire.*

In any case, the measure of the distance separating the political-social and artistic conditions of the Mentuhotep era, and the era of a Twelfth Dynasty ruler such as Sesostris III, is particularly well evinced by a comparison of their respective statues; the lively, aggressive and semi-'barbaric' effigy of the Theban nomarch contrasts dramatically with the statue of Sesostris, built according to traditional rules, as though Chephren had been reborn. Nevertheless, the passage of history applies also to Pharaohs, and the freer idiom which typifies Middle Kingdom art gives to the face of Sesostris greater characterization and living tension.

Artistically, the Middle Kingdom marks the triumph of local idioms. With the fall of political centralization, art too became less centralized, making for a freer style, less in conformity with standardized patterns. The chromatic scale too was enriched with new shades of colour, gaining release from the monotony of the few conventional tones previously allowed.

Less submissive than their predecessors to the magical powers of the tomb, the nomarchs of the period meant their mortuary monuments to serve as glorification of their achievements and as reminders for their descendants of their meritorious actions.

Thus all figures in their tombs appear in a given space and time, with date and place accurately indicated.

The descriptive and commemorative style which these Pharaohs employed appears only in the decoration of their great temples. But like the sceptical poet mentioned earlier who wrote the *Song of the Harpist at the Feast*, the nomarchs preferred terrestrial fame and glory to resurrection.

With the Thirteenth and Fourteenth Dynasties,

internal disorders started anew and the authority of the state grew so weak that Egypt lay practically helpless in the face of the invasion by the Hyksos or 'Shepherd kings', a Semitic people probably from Asia Minor. Thus, foreign domination put an end to the Middle Kingdom.

THE NEW EMPIRE

Like the fabulous phoenix with its many lives, Egypt rose rejuvenated from her ashes for the second time, her finest artistic period yet to come. Once again, Theban princes led the national revival, and it was a Theban dynasty (the Eighteenth) which restored Pharaonic authority and renewed the ancient tradition of the king's divine descent.

Thebes now became the splendid spiritual and religious capital of the New Empire, as well as the political capital until the transfer of the imperial residence to Tanis in the eastern part of the Delta, under the Nineteenth Dynasty.

The ancient Theban deity, Ammon, was raised to the status of national god, at the apex of the state religion. With a typical syncretic procedure beloved by Egyptian theology, Ammon assimilated the other supreme deities – the Memphite god Ptah and the sun-god Râ, head of the Heliopolis Ennead, who was the national deity at the time of the great pyramids – assuming the new form of Ammon-Râ.

'Thebes was in existence before any other place . . . the creation of the world and of the gods took place at Thebes and was the work of its god Ammon' states a papyrus written at the time of Ramses II. Thus was created and entrenched the tradition of the primacy

43   *Tuthmosis III (left) and Amenophis II (right) depicted in the guise of suppliants tendering gifts. New Empire. Egyptian Museum, Cairo, and Egyptian Museum, Turin.*

43 *Tuthmosis III* (left) and *Amenophis II* (right) *depicted in the guise of suppliants tendering gifts*. New Empire. Egyptian Museum, Cairo, and Egyptian Museum, Turin.

The Pharaohs of the Eighteenth Dynasty often liked to be portrayed as suppliants on their knees. In certain cases, their figures, constructed with a rigid symmetry, display a certain harshness.

44 *Tuthmosis IV with his mother Teo.* New Empire. Egyptian Museum. Cairo.

This granite group, taken from Karnak, depicts Pharaoh Tuthmosis IV and his mother, Queen Teo, who ranked immediately after him, as the highest dignitary. The woman's hair is done in the 'vulture' style, a divine symbol of her regal power.

45 *The daughters of Amenophis IV*. New Empire. Ashmolean Museum, Oxford.

A fragment from a fresco found at Tell el-Amarna depicts the two daughters of Amenophis IV. The still immature gracefulness of the two little girls is in contrast with their distorted heads.

46 *Fresco from the tomb of Nebamon*, near Thebes (detail). New Empire. British Museum, London.

Two slave-girls move gracefully in the dance. The flute-player is painted frontally, an unusual practice in Egyptian painting.

47 *Fresco from the tomb of Nebamon*, near Thebes (detail). New Empire. British Museum, London.

Graceful young ladies exchange flowers at a feast. They are dressed in elegant *toilettes*. Their head-dress, adorned with a profusion of ribbons and jewels, is crowned with a cone of solid perfume.

48 *Funeral chapel of Tuthmosis III*. New Empire.

The sides of the chapel are painted in a yellowish tone, on which inscriptions and figures alternate. The figures are drawn rather schematically and rigidly.

44 *Tuthmosis IV with his mother Teo. New Empire. Egyptian Museum, Cairo.*

45 *The daughters of Amenophis IV. New Empire. Ashmolean Museum, Oxford,*

46   *Fresco from the tomb of Nebamon, near Thebes (detail). New Empire.
British Museum, London.*

47   *Fresco from the tomb of Nebamon, near Thebes (detail). New Empire.
British Museum, London.*

48   *Funeral chapel of Tuthmosis III. New Empire.*

of Thebes and its god, legitimating the authority of the Theban Pharaoh, engendered by Ammon, the most ancient and venerable of gods, and his divine wife, the queen-mother.

At Karnak, the successive efforts of generations of Egyptians raised the state temple, the assembly-ground of all the divinities of Egypt, each one of which was lodged in its separate chapel. This was the greatest effort made to unify the complex, difficult and contradictory Egyptian religion, tied to the particularism of local divinities, in which only Isis and Osiris (though not always) had enjoyed a national following since remote prehistoric times.

At the start of the New Empire, the figurative arts followed the traces of the tradition inaugurated during the preceding epoch.

The mortuary temple of Queen Hatshepsut at Deir el-Bahari, not very far from that of Mentuhotep, contains rooms with porches, terraces, flights of steps towards the rock and so forth, and also blends suggestively with the surrounding landscape.

The tombs of succeeding Theban Pharaohs were likewise dug out of the rock (following the example given by the nomarchs of the Middle Kingdom) to obtain extra protection against the hatred of enemies – a violated tomb could imperil the eternal 'rebirth' of the dead person. 'May the crocodile in the water and the snake on the ground be against anyone who tries to do any harm to this tomb'.

Egyptian rulers also relied on magic spells for protection against all who would endanger their eternal security. But magic spells did not save Hatshepsut from the hatred of her husband and step-brother Tuthmosis III whom she had dethroned. Nor did

49   *Fresco from the tomb of Horemheb. New Empire. Valley of
the Kings.*

50 *Fresco from the tomb of Nebamon, near Thebes. New Empire. British Museum, London.*

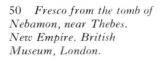

51   *Harp figurehead. New Empire. Louvre Museum, Paris.*

52 *Head of Nefertiti. New Empire. Berlin, Ehemals Staatliche Museen.*

49 *Fresco from the tomb of Horemheb*. New Empire. Valley of the Kings.

Four years after the death of Tutenkhamen, an official of plebeian origin named Horemheb gained the throne. In this fresco, the new sovereign receives the insignia of authority from Isis.

50 *Fresco from the tomb of Nebamon,* near Thebes. New Empire. British Museum, London.

That we possess the frescoes from Nebamon's tomb at all is a miracle, as the colours used are extremely fragile. The artist who painted them used crushed straw, palm-fibre brushes and sea-shells to dilute his colours.

51 *Harp figurehead*. New Empire. Louvre Museum, Paris.

Accurate modelling and detailed attention paid to a subject's physical and moral characteristics are hallmarks of artefacts from Tell el-Amarna.

52 *Head of Nefertiti*. New Empire. Ehemals Staatliche Museen, Berlin.

This painted limestone bust reproduces the delicate and enigmatic features of Nefertiti, wife of Ikhnaton. Her intense eyes, soft but imperious mouth, pure profile and long neck, all combine to produce a splendid artefact.

53 *Offerings for Aton,* limestone relief from Tell el-Amarna. New Empire. Egyptian Museum, Cairo.

The image of Aton, the solar disc, figuratively expresses the new religious conception proclaimed by Amenophis IV. The sun sends forth its life-giving rays to Pharaoh. The hieroglyphic symbol for the word 'life' is inscribed at the end of the sun's rays.

54 *Amenophis IV with his wife*. New Empire. Louvre Museum, Paris.

Amenophis IV (or Ikhnaton) and Nefertiti are depicted holding hands in accordance with the widespread Amarnian iconographical practice, which delighted in scenes of affectionate family life.

53 *Offerings for Aton, limestone relief from Tell el-Amarna. New Empire. Egyptian Museum, Cairo.*

54   *Amenophis IV (Ikhnaton) with his wife. New Empire. Louvre Museum, Paris.*

it protect the heretic Ikhnaton from the ire of the priests of Ammon, at the end of the Eighteenth Dynasty.

The beginning of the New Empire witnessed a revival of the *joie de vivre* which characterized the moderate 'realism' of Middle Kingdom artefacts. To this was added a delicacy, an exquisite taste for precious decoration and refined elegance. This applied especially to wall paintings in tombs; such decoration was embellished, enlivened, rescued from its conventional monotony and sometimes completely altered from the canon.

In a fresco from the splendid tomb of Nebamon (one of the all-time masterpieces of Egyptian painting), the flute-player providing music for the feast is depicted facing forwards. This was an iconographical revolution, which is further emphasized by the splendid adjacent figures of two young girls dancing in a delicate counterpoint of gestures and attitudes, and painted in profile.

Further on, Nebamon is shown hunting in a swamp, in a paradisial landscape, dotted with lotus-flowers and fantastic birds, almost as if it came from some late-Gothic bestiary.

The descriptive realism, with its emphasis on actual everyday events, which characterized the tombs of the ancient nomarchs, is seen once again in Queen Hatshepsut's mortuary temple. The description it gives of the Land of Punt is so detailed that it includes observations made by an expedition to that distant and exotic land concerning its inhabitants, their dwellings, the plants growing there and so forth, thus providing a permanent graphic record.

This analytical and narrative realism was typical of

55   *Tutankhamen's second coffin. New Empire. Egyptian Museum, Cairo.*

55 *Tutankhamen's second coffin.* New Empire. Egyptian Museum, Cairo.
A sarcophagus containing three priceless coffins in human form housed the young Pharaoh. A gold mask bearing his features covered his face.

56 *Seat inlaid with mother-of-pearl, hard stones and coloured glass.* New Empire. Egyptian Museum, Cairo.
Never was there a luckier find than that of Tutankhamen's tomb, which was filled with innumerable treasure affectionately deposited around his body by his young widow.

57 *Gold-plated shrine.* New Empire. Egyptian Museum, Cairo.
Displaying the most refined workmanship, this shrine from Tutankhamen's treasure is shaped like a chapel and is entirely covered by a thin sheet of gold. The graceful scenes engraved on the thin gold casing depict carefree moments in the life of Tutankhamen and his young wife.

58 *Fresco from Tutankhamen's tomb.* New Empire. Valley of the Kings.
Tutankhamen's tomb and the objects found in his treasure are linked in the popular mind with an utterly unfounded legend about an alleged curse bringing death to anyone meddling with them.

59 *Small painted wood coffer.* New Empire. Egyptian Museum, Cairo.
In Tutankhamen's treasure, even the most common domestic objects have been produced with the utmost refinement and attention to detail, providing striking proof of the prodigious skill displayed by the craftsmen of the Theban Court. The minutely detailed paintings decorating this wooden coffer are unparalleled in Egyptian art.

56　*Seat inlaid with mother-of-pearl, hard stones and coloured glass. New Empire. Egyptian Museum, Cairo.*

57   *Gold-plated shrine. New Empire. Egyptian Museum, Cairo.*

58   *Fresco from the tomb of Tutankhamen. New Empire.*
Valley of the Kings.

commemorative scenes ordered by Pharaohs to celebrate their deeds, so that the people should know about them and remember them. It was also destined to make all Egyptians aware of the might of their Empire. All the great temples of the New Empire – Karnak, Abydos, Abu Simbel and Medinet Habu – are richly adorned with such scenes illustrating for all to see the power and the glory of the Nineteenth Dynasty Pharaohs.

Tuthmosis III, however, chose to leave in his Festival Hall at Karnak a singularly detailed portrayal of the animals and plants brought back from an expedition to Syria, in such profusion that the area is now known as the Botanic Gardens.

Construction of the Karnak complex was begun fairly early during the New Empire. Former constructions certainly do not compare with the incredible gran-

59   *Small painted wooden coffer. New Empire. Egyptian Museum, Cairo.*

deur of the buildings erected under the Nineteenth Dynasty, the era of the Ramessides.

Eighteenth Dynasty taste tended, in any event, more to refinement than to grandeur. For instance, Amenophis I ordered the building of an alabaster chapel, and Hatshepsut raised two obelisks in red Aswan granite (obelisks are typical Egyptian monuments symbolizing the rays of the sun). The Festival Hall of Tuthmosis III imitates the shape and structure of a tent. The capitals of its columns are of a composite type incorporating various flowers, both in bloom and in bud, and the decorative effect is striking.

This artistic trend was interrupted at the end of the Eighteenth Dynasty by a complete artistic revolution promoted by Amenophis IV, which marks a sharp break in the course of Egyptian art. This revolution lasted all through this Pharaoh's reign, but was

then overwhelmed by the wave of reaction.

Possibly disquieted by the excessive power achieved by the priests of Ammon, Amenophis decided to abolish his cult and that of the other Egyptian gods, replacing them by a single god. This was an unprecedented step in the history of Egyptian religion, although a form of monotheism had long been practised by the cultured upper classes, to whom Râ, or rather his representatives, would say: 'I am a god with many names and many forms, and my form is in every god'. The new god was Aton, the life-giving sun. Here was no longer an abstract deity, a concept or the dogmatic and intellectual transposition of some natural or spiritual force, but an entirely physical, fully visible and even tangible god. To represent Aton, Amenophis selected the most material aspect of the sun – the solar disc. In pictorial representation, each sun-ray ends with a hand, and each hand is marked with a hieroglyphic with the meaning of 'life'. 'You appear beautiful on the horizon of the sky, You the living sun, creator of life . . . And you flood every land with your beauty . . . When you set on the western horizon, The earth lies as dead in the darkness. When dawn comes and you rise on the horizon . . . The Two Lands happily awaken. By yourself, you have millions of aspects. You are life itself and we live for you . . .' The famous *Hymn to the Sun* composed by Ikhnaton is an impassioned paean to creation itself, hailing life and oblivious of death.

In order to demonstrate unmistakably his break with tradition, Amenophis IV moved his capital from Thebes to Akhetaton (near present-day Tell el-Amarna, on the Nile north of Thebes), a new city founded to mark the change. He also changed his own name to Ikhnaton – 'He-in-whom-Aton-is-satisfied'. As regards the representational arts, the Amarnian epoch marks without exaggeration the most complete and advanced attempt at realism ever made in the ancient Near East. This was the consequence of the complete laicization which Ikhnaton imposed upon the society of his time. 'Truth' was now the dominant feature of representations. No longer were personalities idealized, but ruthlessly and impiously shown with all their physical malformations.

Nevertheless, because its origin lay not in craftsmen's workshops but in legal reforms imposed from above, the Amarnian revolution did not achieve all its possibilities and traditional representational formulas were not much modified. Thus Bek, Ikhnaton's chief sculptor, could rightly call himself 'His Majesty's pupil', as everything new that appeared in Egyptian art was due to the King's direct suggestion.

Painters and sculptors have left us artefacts depicting private and intimate moments of the serene day-to-day life led by the King and his wife. The sculptor's chisel, in its search for character, has dug skilfully into their faces, deepening wrinkles and enhancing lineaments. And in at least one case, it created a great masterpiece in which elegance and naturalism are fused. This is the head of Nefertiti, the wife of Ikhnaton. It would be difficult to find, prior to the Ptolemaic era, another likeness so alive and sensitive, so realistic and at the same time so delicate.

But Ikhnaton's reforms were short-lived and did not survive him. The cult of Ammon was restored. Akhetaton was abandoned, the temple of Aton, with its courtyards open to the sun, the name of the schismatic Pharaoh erased from all monuments, and his memory damned for all eternity.

Thebes rose once again as the capital and centre of worship.

'Your city is still in existence, but the city of he who insulted you has perished. The sun of he who does not know you has set, but the sun of he who does know you is shining in splendour. The sanctuary of he who harmed you lies in darkness, and the whole earth is full of light'.

In the wake of the priesthood of Ammon, some modern scholars have also described Ikhnaton as a visionary and fanatic, while his attempt at complete laicization seems utterly incredible when related to the beliefs and culture of the time, so unused to materialistic ideas.

Figurative arts likewise abandoned the themes celebrated in the Amarnian epoch. In the tomb of General Horemheb (who subsequently became Pharaoh), the oldest decorations are in the Amarnian style, but following the death of the schismatic Ikhnaton, the tomb was completed on traditional lines in the pre-Amarnian style. This is not an isolated example, and should not cause surprise, as tombs were obviously built during the lifetime of their prospective occupant (dying without one's tomb being ready would have been prejudicial to Osirian resurrection) and they reflect the ups and downs of successive political and artistic changes.

Echoes of the Amarnian period, however exceptional, can be found during the brief reign of Ikhnaton's successor, his son-in-law Tutankhaton, who, following the Theban restoration, changes his name to Tutankhamen. This ruler is now one of the best-known of Egyptian Pharaohs thanks to the circumstances in

60 *Tutankhamen's Throne.*
New Empire. Egyptian
Museum, Cairo.

60 *Tutankhamen's Throne*. New Empire. Egyptian Museum, Cairo.
Carved wood throne, covered with a sheet of gold, with many-coloured inlays in glass, majolica, silver and hard stones. Note on the sides the unfurled wings of two deities, symbolizing the double crown of Upper and Lower Egypt.

61 *Detail of Tutankhamen's Throne*. New Empire. Egyptian Museum, Cairo.
The back of the throne, with exquisite workmanship, charmingly depicts the royal couple in a moment of relaxation, watched over by Aton.

62 *Golden base of Tutankhamen's second coffin*. New Empire. Egyptian Museum, Cairo.
Isis unfurls her wings protectively. The hieroglyphics in the background are good wishes for the repose of the king.

63 *'Salt' Head*. New Empire. Louvre Museum, Paris.
The dating of the 'Salt' Head is uncertain, but its realism would be inconceivable prior to the Amarnian revolution.

64 *Dancer*. New Empire. Egyptian Museum, Turin.
Beginning as a religious rite which turned into entertainment, dancing was a natural part of all ceremonies, funerals, feasts and banquets. This stone fragment shows the graceful and agile profile of an acrobatic dancer.

65 *Alabaster group*. New Empire. Louvre Museum, Paris.
The attitude of the group is pleasingly asymmetrical, and the scribe is carved with great freedom and vivacity.

66 *Starting point of the Avenue of the Rams, and details of pylons*. Temple of Ammon at Karnak. New Empire.
In many New Empire temples, two stone structures flank each side of the main entrance, in symbolic evocation of the mountains out of which the sun rises each morning.

61   *Detail of Tutankhamen's Throne. New Empire.*
Egyptian Museum, Cairo.

62   *Golden base of Tutankhamen's second coffin. New*
Empire. Egyptian Museum, Cairo.

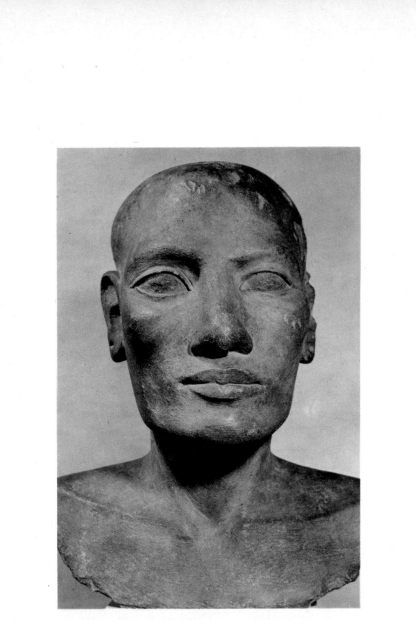

63 *'Salt' Head. New Empire. Louvre Museum, Paris.*

64   *Dancer. New Empire. Egyptian Museum, Turin.*

65 *Alabaster group. New Empire.*
Louvre Museum, Paris.

66   *Starting point of the Avenue of the Rams and details of pylons. Temple of Ammon at Karnak. New Empire.*

which his tomb was discovered. It is one of the very few to have escaped the depredations of grave-robbers and it was found intact by the British archaeologist Howard Carter. The fabulous treasure which the tomb contained conveys the measure of the skill and refinement attained by Egyptian craftsmen working in the decorative arts, combining the utmost magnificence with the utmost comfort (not for nothing did goldsmiths boast a higher social status than painters). Nevertheless, even this treasure provides only a pale idea of what must have been the mortuary fittings of much more powerful and renowned Pharaohs who did not die young, such as Tuthmosis, Seti and Ramses.

Among the innumerable treasures found in the tomb, the most striking is Ikhnaton's throne, on the back of which a typically Amarnian scene is depicted, showing the affectionate conversation of the royal couple in a serene and delicate intimacy.

With Horemheb, Tutankhamen's successor, Egypt resumed her penetration of the Near East (Palestine and Syria), which had begun under Tuthmosis III but had been interrupted by Ikhnaton. The latter, owing to his preoccupations with internal reforms, had largely neglected his country's foreign policy and its interests in neighbouring lands.

Egyptian predominance in the region was being challenged by the Hittites who had now become the strongest power in the Near East. Ramses II defeated them in the great battle of Kadesh, and established permanent Egyptian overlordship over the Asiatic coasts. The marriage between the victorious Ramses and the daughter of the Hittite king consolidated even further the position reached by Egypt, which had never before known such power.

Ramses II was the greatest builder of the New Empire. During the Eighteenth Dynasty, Tuthmosis III and Amenophis III were sovereigns more interested in the construction of Karnak and Luxor, two temple complexes linked by a paved avenue lined with sphinxes (lions with rams' heads) sacred to Ammon. With the Nineteenth Dynasty, the building programme promoted by the kings reached unprecedented proportions. It seemed that by implementing this type of artistic policy, it was intended to obliterate completely any recollection of the Amarnian period and the ideas promoted and advocated by Ikhnaton. At Abydos, the city sacred to Osiris, Seti I launched yet another temple project, improved and completed by his son Ramses II. But it is the building programme undertaken by the latter Pharaoh which stylistically characterizes Nineteenth Dynasty architecture, with its incredible magnificence, immensity of proportion, and unrestrained display of naked power and uncontrolled majesty.

The fabulous Hypostyle Hall at Karnak (a gigantic forest of stone pillars), the mortuary temple or Ramesseum at Thebes, the temples of Abu Simbel – these works arouse echoes of the gloomy conclusions reached by Herodotus in respect of the Labyrinth of Meride:

'Superior to any description . . . superior to human scale . . . if we assembled together all the buildings and works of art in Greece, the amount of labour involved and their total cost of construction would prove to be very much inferior'.

This stylistic tradition continues with the temple of Medinet Habu, near Thebes, built by Ramses III, the last great ruler of the New Empire. This temple

67   *Fresco from the tomb of Sennedjem at Deir el-Medineh, near Thebes.*
New Empire.

Outer casing of the sarcophagus of Chons, from a tomb at Deir el-Medineh.
ew Empire.

67 *Fresco from the tomb of Sennedjem* at Deir el-Medineh, near Thebes. New Empire.

The small valley of Deir el-Medineh is the resting place of those who lavished their arts and skills for the embellishment of the tombs in the nearby Valley of the Kings. The tomb of the craftsman Sennedjem, a detail of which is shown here, is one of the best preserved.

68 *Outer casing of the sarcophagus of Chons*, from a tomb at Deir el-Medineh. New Empire.

New Empire rulers and officials were not content with a single coffin. Their mummy had to be protected by a whole series of casings, up to seven or eight, depending on their importance. The outermost sarcophagus usually consists of an immense painted wood chest, decorated with excerpts of religious-funerary texts and the figures of protective deities.

69 *Colossal statue of Ramses II*. New Empire.

A tremendous work of monumental sculpture located near one of the temples built in Nubia.

70 *Façade of the 'Little Temple' at Abu Simbel*. New Empire. Almasy Photo.

Not far from the cliff-side temple of Ramses II at Abu Simbel, stands a smaller temple dedicated to the powerful goddess Hathor as well as Pharaoh's wife Nefertari. The temple's façade is decorated with colossal statues.

71 *Façade of the cliff-side temple of Ramses II* at Abu Simbel. New Empire. Almasy Photo.

The name of Ramses II is linked to a series of grandiose structures scattered throughout Egypt. Here the Pharaoh had a sanctuary excavated from the mountain of Abu Simbel. Its façade is decorated by four gigantic statues.

69   *Colossal statue of Ramses II. New Empire.*

70 *Façade of the 'Little Temple' at Abu Simbel. New Empire.*

71   *Façade of the cliff-side temple of Ramses II at Abu Simbel. New Empire.*

is constructed more like an impregnable fortress than a religious shrine.

Amenophis IV-Ikhnaton proved to be a true prophet. The dedication with which successive Pharaohs glorified the power of Ammon continually boosted the power of his priesthood. The post of High Priest of Ammon became hereditary, and the incumbent became so powerful as to supersede Pharaoh's authority and rule over the whole of Upper Egypt. Once again, the land underwent one of its cyclical crises, and the country's unity was only restored with the curbing of priestly power through the efforts of a dynasty of Libyan soldiers – the Twenty-Second. With the Libyan period, Pharaonic art can be said to have reached practically the end of its most vivid and original motifs.

In fact, apart from certain refined sculptures in bronze, in which the skilful inlay of precious metals – gold and silver – vitreous pastes and hard stones, gives a particular charm, a trend was now growing simply to imitate works of the past, especially those of the Middle Kingdom.

The Libyan Dynasties (the Twenty-Second and Twenty-Third) were unable to preserve the unity of Egypt for more than two centuries. Even before their rule was over, the land was already divided into many separate small states which were *de facto* independent. Their independence was to end only at the end of the eighth century BC when Nubians from the south imposed a new unity on the whole of Egypt for a few decades.

72 *Bronze statuette of Queen Karomama.*
Period of Decline. Louvre Museum, Paris.

73   *Female figure –*
wood. Period of Decline.
British Museum, London.

74　*The goddess Sekhmet. Period of Decline. British Museum, London.*

72 *Bronze statuette of Queen Karomama*. Period of Decline. Louvre Museum, Paris.
Karomama's tiny face, firm glance and graceful bearing live again in this gold-inlaid bronze statuette.

73 *Wooden female figure*. Period of Decline. British Museum, London.
The holes drilled in the skull of this Negroid servant-girl were for a wig.

74 *The goddess Sekhmet*. Period of Decline. British Museum, London.
Sekhmet has a lion's head, and surmounted solar disc.

75 *Gilded and decorated funerary mask*. Greek period. Egyptian Museum, Cairo.
Even when Egypt was witnessing the rise of a new civilization, the old local traditions persisted.

76 *Papyrus*. New Empire. Egyptian Museum, Cairo.
A papyrus giving details of religious beliefs and funeral rites was deposited in the tombs of the wealthy.

77 *Cube-statue*. Period of Decline. Egyptian Museum, Cairo.
Cube-statues are a constant factor in Egyptian art, from the Old Kingdom to the Period of Decline.

78 *Statue of Governor Mentemhet*. Period of Decline. Egyptian Museum, Cairo.
This black granite statue depicts the high official Mentemhet during the era of the last Ethiopian kings (eighth century BC).

79–80 *Painted reliefs from the tomb of Seti I*. New Empire. Valley of the Kings.
The tomb of Seti I in the Valley of the Kings attests to the wealth of the era. These painted bas-reliefs are of extraordinary beauty.

75   *Gilded and decorated funerary mask. Greek period.*
Egyptian Museum, Cairo.

76   *Papyrus. New Empire. Egyptian Museum, Cairo.*

77   *Cube-statue. Period of Decline. Egyptian Museum,*
Cairo.

78   *Statue of Governor Mentemhet. Period of Decline.*
Egyptian Museum, Cairo.

79　*Painted relief from the tomb of Seti I. New Empire. Va¹¹ey of the Kings.*

80   *Painted relief from the tomb of Seti I. New Empire. Valley
of the Kings.*

THE PERIOD OF DECLINE

The final centuries of the millennial history of ancient Egypt are a continuous alternation of foreign domination and national revolts. A constant factor, however, was the general respect in which Egyptian traditions and beliefs were held. Thus in 332 BC, when Alexander had completed the conquest of the entire country, he hastened to the oracle of Ammon at Siwa, to be declared the latter's beloved son. Likewise the Greek Ptolemies felt themselves to be in every respect the descendants of the divine Pharaohs and their natural heirs.

The struggle between the Nubian princes and the Egyptian national element led by the Lords of Saïs, backed by Assurbanipal, the Assyrian overlord of the Delta, ended with the advent of the Saïte King Psammetichus to the throne. The Twenty-Sixth Dynasty was the last true independent dynasty in Egypt and it revived for a while the Pharaonic and imperial dreams of the New Empire.

But the heroic days of Ramses II could not return. Nebuchadnezzer defeated Pharaoh Necho's army at Carchemish on the Euphrates. The might of Persia, which was spreading throughout the entire Near East, finally brought to an end any dreams of Egyptian revival and overlordship over Syria and Palestine.

Saïte art represents one of the many 'revivals' or 'restorations' of the ancient forms, which were always attempted every time policy dictated a return to archaic sources, a recall to the traditions of the past, not deeply felt but simply copied in block. Copies of antiques are a characteristic of Saïte art.

But the importance of the Decline in artistic terms is

81 *Illustrations from a Book of the Dead. New Empire. British Museum,
London.*

82   *Fresco from the tomb of Ramses VI. New Empire. Valley of the Kings.*

83   *Painted relief from the tomb of Amonchopeshefu, near Thebes. New Empire.*

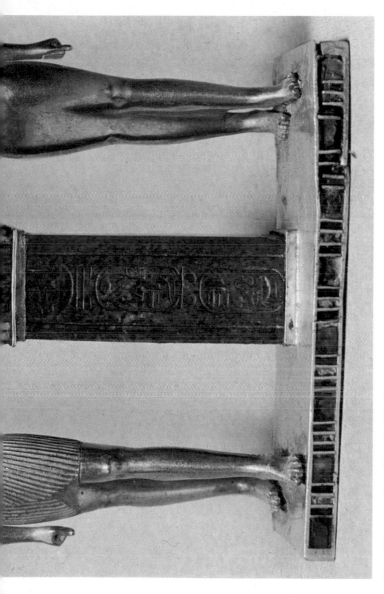

84 Osirian pendant. Period of Decline. Louvre Museum, Paris.

81 *Illustrations from a Book of the Dead.* New Empire. British Museum, London.

Egyptian frescoes, paintings and reliefs often illustrate the culminating moment of funeral ceremonies – the opening of the mouth. This singular rite, which was performed by touching the dead man's mouth with a particular ritual instrument, symbolized his resurrection to the new life beyond the tomb.

82 *Fresco from the tomb of Ramses VI.* New Empire. Valley of the Kings.

The scene, framed by the body of Nut, the personification of the celestial vault, represents the nocturnal journeyings of the sun.

83 *Painted relief from the tomb of Amonchopeshefu*, near Thebes. New Empire.

The geometrical-decorative taste of the ancient Egyptians is obvious in this composition of two symmetrical figures – Ramses III and the divine Hathor – enlivened by brilliant colouring.

84 *Osirian pendant.* Period of Decline. Louvre Museum, Paris.

This four-inch-high gold and lapis-lazuli pendant is a splendid representation of the god Osiris depicted between his wife Isis and his son Horus.

85 *Fresco from the tomb of Ramses VI.* New Empire. Valley of the Kings.

Illustrations taken from the Book of the Dead. The style of the figures recalls that in illustrations found on papyri.

86 *Detail from the statue of Ramses II.* New Empire. Egyptian Museum, Turin.

This black granite statue of Ramses II wearing the 'azure' crown, is a masterpiece of Nineteenth Dynasty sculpture.

85 *Fresco from the tomb of Ramses VI. New Empire. Valley of the Kings.*

86 *Detail from the statue of Ramses II. New Empire.*
Egyptian Museum, Turin.

of another nature and lies in the dualistic fracture that split Egyptian art from the Nubian era onwards. The priestly caste remained tied to archaism and a resumption of traditional themes. The cultured classes advocated realistic portraiture and individualistic representation of subjects.

The impressive portrayal of the official Mentemhet, Governor of Thebes at the time of the last Ethiopian kings (eighth century BC), are the masterpieces of this trend.

The Saïte restoration naturally favoured the taste for the archaic, imitation and the search for the antique. In 525 BC, at Pelusium, the Persian Cambyses defeated and killed Psammetichus III. Egyptian independence was once again regained prior to the final reconquest by Artaxerxes III (341 BC), and the Macedonian invasion. But there would be no more 'revivals' on the Saïte model.

At this period, the artistic trend was veering to realism. Splendid examples are the so-called 'Green Heads' in dark-green granite, likenesses of great expressive force and character. Notwithstanding their modernity of conception, here too we can clearly perceive the characteristic and traditional Egyptian keynote of restraint which always prevented the attainment of an integral sense of realism.

The finest of the Green Heads date from the Ptolemaic period, but with their resemblance to likenesses made in Republican Rome, it is only with difficulty that they could be classed as 'Egyptian'.

With the Ptolemies, Greek culture penetrated Egypt, co-existing but not integrating with native culture. Alexandria remained one of the main centres of Hellenism, while the Ptolemies did their utmost to

87   *Basalt torso of a royal statue. Period of Decline. Louvre Museum, Paris.*

88 *Head of a Pharaoh. Period of Decline. Ny Carlsberg Glyptotek, Copenhagen.*

89 *Bronze statuette of the goddess Bast. Roman period. British Museum, London.*

90   *Fragment of relief. Period of Decline. Egyptian Museum,*
Turin.

145

87 *Basalt torso of a royal statue.* Period of Decline. Louvre Museum, Paris.

It is not known for certain whether this torso represents a Pharaoh of the Twenty-fifth Dynasty, or whether it dates from the time of the Ptolemies. The shiny and smooth surface is characteristic of the latter period.

88 *Head of Pharaoh.* Period of Decline. Ny Carlsberg Glyptotek, Copenhagen.

This royal head may portray one of the princes who tried to overthrow Persian domination between 404 and 341 BC.

89 *Bronze statuette of the goddess Bast.* Roman period. British Museum, London.

The cat-goddess Bast was worshipped in the city of Bubastis. Animal cults developed during the Period of Decline.

90 *Fragment of relief.* Period of Decline. Egyptian Museum, Turin.

Portrayal of the manufacture of lily ointment. The figures are animated by a rather good sense of line.

91 *Bronze statuette of the god Osiris.* Period of Decline. Louvre Museum, Paris.

Osiris' hands bear his sceptre and whip which are his insignia of power. His head is covered by the crown known as *Atef*, decorated with ostrich feathers, one of the god's iconographical attributes.

92 *Temple of Kom-Ombo.* Anteroom. Greek period.

The best-preserved part of this temple is the anteroom. Some of its columns reproduce the classical Egyptian style. Others show the influence of Hellenistic decoration, especially in their capitals.

93 *Detail of a column from the temple of Kom-Ombo.* Greek period.

The remaining sections are covered with inscribed decorations consisting of hieroglyphics and pictures, as well as traces of paint.

91   *Bronze statuette of the god Osiris. Period of Decline. Louvre Museum, Paris.*

147

92 *Temple of Kom-Ombo. Anteroom. Greek
period.*

   93 *Detail of a column from the temple of Kom-Ombo. Greek
period.*

act as genuine Pharaohs. The Egyptian element remained dominant in official art. Royal statues preserved the usual rigidity, although faces had a trace of Hellenistic beauty. Even Rome failed to destroy traditional Egyptian culture.

When the Emperor Hadrian had a statue of his favourite Antinoos erected in Egypt, he insisted on the 'Egyptian' style. It is only the torso with its greater anatomical detail which shows we are now in the second century AD, and that Hadrian is not Chephren. It was only when true Graeco-Roman portraits appeared on mummy-cases (the famous Faiyûm portraits) that it could be said that Egyptian art, in the sense of transmitting to posterity traditional themes and formal conventions, was really finished.

Herodotus began his description of Egypt by remarking that this nation 'offers a great number of extraordinary things and possesses marvels which words are powerless to describe'. It is fitting to conclude this study with this judgment by the great Greek historian, because his wonder and admiration reflect the exceptional nature of a unique artistic and cultural achievement.

CHRONOLOGICAL OUTLINE OF EGYPTIAN HISTORY

The preservation of a certain number of original records giving lists of kings (such as the temple of Tuthmosis III at Karnak, the walls of the temple of Seti I at Abydos, and the fragmentary *Papyrus of the Kings*, now in the Turin Egyptian Museum, which lists the kings from the First Dynasty to the New Empire), or other records (such as the Palermo Stone and the Cairo fragment, which record the most important events in Egyptian history up to the Fifth Dynasty), as well as histories and literary sources (such as the History of Egypt written by the priest Manetho under Ptolemy II Philadelphus towards 280 BC, only fragments of which remain), provide a reasonably detailed outline of the succession of events in the history of ancient Egypt.

From Manetho derives the still accepted convention of dividing the Pharaohs who ruled over Egypt into thirty dynasties.

> *Proto-historic Period :* Dynasties I and II.
> Chronology: Approximately 3200–2780 BC (according to others approximately 2950–2660 BC).
> Capital: Thinis.
> Necropolis: Abydos.
> *Old Kingdom :* Dynasties III to VI.
> Chronology: Approximately 2780–2280 BC (according to others approximately 2660–2160 BC).
> Capital: Memphis.
> Necropolises: Saqqârah, Gizeh, Memphis.
> Dynasty III (approx. 2780–2680 BC – both here and elsewhere we quote only the earlier dates proposed by scholars).

Dynasty IV (approx. 2680–2560 BC). The time of the great pyramids.

Dynasty V (approx. 2560–2420 BC). Together with the previous period, represents the Golden Age of Old Kingdom art. This is the heyday of the Heliopolis Sun Cult. The Sun-God Râ becomes the supreme deity of Egypt and Pharaoh proclaims himself his son.

Dynasty VI (approx. 2420–2280 BC). Officials and nomarchs become increasingly powerful. The Old Kingdom comes to an end amid social unrest and clashes between local potentates.

First Interregnum : Dynasties VII to X.

Chronology: Approximately 2280–2052 BC (according to others approximately 2160–2040 BC). Pharaonic authority is practically non-existent. Various local lords are dominant. The most important centre in Lower and Middle Egypt is Heracleopolis.

Middle Kingdom : Dynasties XI and XII.

Chronology: Approximately 2134–1778 BC (according to others 1785). This chronology also includes the reigns of the sovereigns of Thebes, before they became lords of all Egypt.

Capital: Thebes, subsequently Memphis.

Dynasty XI: Approximately 2134–1991 BC.

Dynasty XII: Approximately 1991–1778 BC.

Local tendencies are dominant in the figurative arts. Mortuary temple of Mentuhotep at Deir el-Bahari, and tombs of the various nomarchs.

Second interregnum : Dynasties XIII to XVII.

Chronology: Approximately 1778–1557 BC. Decay of the state and another breakdown of Egyptian unity. As in the previous interregnum, grave cultural decadence. From the XVth Dynasty, Egypt submits to the foreign rule of the Hyksos, a Semitic people.

New Empire : Dynasties XVIII to XX.

Chronology: 1557–1185 BC.

Capital: Thebes. Under the XIXth Dynasty, Tanis.

Necropolises: Mainly the Valley of the Kings, near Thebes. Ahmose, Lord of Thebes, drives the Hyksos out and again unites Egypt.

Dynasty XVIII: 1557–1304 BC:

Amenophis I (1532–1304 BC).

Tuthmosis I and II (1511–1490 BC)

Hatshepsut (approx. 1490–1470 BC)

Tuthmosis III (1490–1437 BC)

Amenophis II (1437–1410 BC)

Amenophis III (1400–1362 BC)

Amenophis IV–Ikhnaton (1362–1334 BC)

Tutankhamen (1346–1334 BC)

Horemheb (1334–1304 BC)

Dynasty XIX: 1304–1200 BC. Era of the Ramessides, and Seti 1 and II.

Dynasty XX: approximately 1200–1185 BC. This is the time of Egypt's greatest political, imperial and artistic splendour.

Third Interregnum : Dynasties XXI to XXV.

Chronology: 1185–655 BC.

Under the XXIst Dynasty, the priesthood of Ammon dominates Thebes. Divine Ammonite State.

Dynasty XXI (950–730 BC). A Libyan military dynasty.

Capital: Bubastis.

Invasion by the Nubians (VIIIth Century), and

by the Assyrians, who conquer Lower Egypt. Assurbanipal sacks Thebes.

Late period : Dynasties XXVI to XXX.

Chronology: 663–332 BC.

Psammetichus, King of Saïs, gains independence from the Assyrians who had supported him against the Nubians.

Dynasty XXVI, a Saïte dynasty, 663–525 BC.

525 BC: Cambyses conquers Egypt.

525–504 BC: Egypt is a Persian satrapy.

Dynasty XXX: 378–341 BC. With Nectanebo, there is a new flowering of Egyptian civilization.

341 BC: Artaxerxes III reconquers Egypt.

332 BC: The Persians are ousted by Alexander the Great. Throughout the entire Decline, the cult of animals becomes highly developed.

Ptolemaic Period : Chronology: 323–30 BC.

31 BC: Battle of Actium.

Egypt becomes a Roman province.

BIBLIOGRAPHY

C. A. BURLAND, *Ancient Egypt, London & New York 1962*

L. COTTRELL, *Egypt, London & New York 1966*

C. DESROCHES-NOBLECOURT, *Ancient Egypt : The New Kingdom and the Amarna Period, London & New York 1961*

C. DESROCHES-NOBLECOURT, *Tutankhamen, London & New York 1963*

F. MALY, *Egyptian Art, New York 1970*

W. M. MULLER, *Egyptian Mythology, New York 1964*

P. P. REISTERER, *Egyptian Cairo Museum, New York 1963–65*

J. VANDIER & M. NAGUIB, *Egypt, Paintings from Tombs and Temples, New York 1954*

J. E. WHITE, *Ancient Egypt, Its Culture & History, New York 1970*

INDEX OF ILLUSTRATIONS

157